LOOK WHAT WHISKERS CAN DO

CAN DO

LOOK What ANIMALS Can Do

LOOK WHAT WHISKERS CAN DO

LOOK What ANIMALS Can Do

BY D. M. SOUZA

Lerner Publications Company · Minneapolis

photo on page 2: **A harbor seal has very long whiskers around its mouth.**

Lerner Publications Company
A division of Lerner Publishing Group
241 First Avenue North
Minneapolis, MN 55401 U.S.A.

Website address: www.lernerbooks.com

Library of Congress Cataloging-in-Publication Data

Souza, D. M. (Dorothy M.)
    Look what whiskers can do / by D. M. Souza.
        p.   cm. — (Look what animals can do)
    Includes bibliographical references and index.
    ISBN-13: 978-0-7613-9459-4 (lib. bdg. : alk. paper)
    ISBN-10: 0-7613-9459-1 (lib. bdg. : alk. paper)
    1. Whiskers—Juvenile literature. I. Title. II. Series: Souza, D. M. (Dorothy M.) Look what animals can do.
    QL942.S58 2007
    599.147—dc22   2005032586

Manufactured in the United States of America
1 2 3 4 5 6 – DP – 12 11 10 09 08 07

TABLE OF CONTENTS

LOOK AROUND. MANY ANIMALS HAVE WHISKERS.

Have you ever noticed a cat's whiskers? The hairs are long and stiff. Each one is two to three times thicker than the animal's other hairs.

Cats depend on their whiskers for many things. Whiskers collect clues about what is around them. They help the animals hunt in the dark.

Whiskers are the most sensitive hairs on a cat's body.

Scientists call whiskers **vibrissae**. The word once meant to shake or vibrate. Whiskers let many animals called **mammals** feel movements or vibrations in both air and water.

Whiskers grow from roots deep below the skin. Blood and nerves surround them. When whiskers pick up movements, nerves sense them.

Whiskers appear on a mammal's cheeks. Some mammals also have them above their eyes and on their chins. A few have them in odd places. Let's look at a few of these whiskers and what they do for their owners.

Tigers have many whiskers on their cheeks, above their eyes, and on their chins.

LIFESAVER

The boat is dark and deserted. A rat is busy searching for food. It cannot see well, so it feels the air with its long whiskers. The animal uses whiskers just as we use hands to find our way in the dark.

Suddenly, the whiskers touch something. They make about eight sweeps in a second. The faster the whiskers move, the more facts they collect. The object is crunchy and tasty.

Rats use their whiskers to help them search for food.

Before the rat can eat it, a giant wave rocks the boat. It sends the rat sliding across the deck. The rat falls into the water.

The animal struggles to keep its nose above water. But another wave tumbles over it. The rat can hardly breathe.

Whiskers come to its rescue. The rat points its stiff whiskers out from the side of its head. Like a life jacket, they hold the top of the animal's head above water. The rat finally reaches shore. Now it must put its whiskers to work finding food again.

A rat's whiskers help keep its head above water while swimming.

SEEING-EYE WHISKERS

Two cats have been blind since birth. But they are clever hunters. Twelve movable whiskers on each cheek tell them about the world around them.

On some days, the animals sit in a field as still as statues. Only their whiskers move. They search for tiny vibrations in the air.

A mouse running near one cat sets off a whisker alarm. The cat's stiff hairs move quickly up and down. They collect clues. In seconds the whiskers send a message to the cat's brain. Mouse!

A cat's whiskers can move up and down. They also move backward and forward.

Whiskers bend forward as the cat pounces. Teeth grasp the mouse tightly around its neck. The cat holds on until its **prey** stops wriggling. Then the cat drops the animal and begins its meal.

When the cats are finished hunting, they return home. They enter the building through a small door. The blind cats use their whiskers to feel their way around. Without bumping into anything, each finds its favorite spot and curls up. Whiskers let blind cats act and move as if they could see.

Whiskers also grow on the back of the cat's front legs. They help in the capture of prey.

UNDERWATER MAGIC

Several large manatees swim slowly through dark waters. They are searching for sea plants off the coast of Florida. They eat plants and grasses as cows do. Some people call manatees sea cows.

Manatees have big noses and small eyes. They cannot see what is in front of them. But their thick lips and about six hundred short whiskers act like sensitive fingers.

When a manatee finds food, its lips and whiskers work together. They pull the plants out of the ground and push them into the manatee's mouth.

Manatees cannot see very well because of their tiny eyes. Their whiskers must lead the way.

19

Now and then, the manatees sink to the sea bottom to rest. They can stay there for as long as twenty minutes. Then they must come up for air.

One animal usually makes the first move. All the others look as if they are still asleep. But slowly the manatees, with their eyes still closed, head for the surface.

Scientists have discovered that hairs on the manatees' bodies are very sensitive. They are whiskerlike. These body whiskers may pick up vibrations. The first manatee swims upward, and the other manatees sense the movement. Then everyone joins in the game of "follow the leader."

When manatees meet, they touch whiskers to find out who's who.

LIVING IN THE DARK

A pocket gopher is moving through its underground home. One long tunnel stretches for about a city block. There are several side tunnels. Some go deeper underground.

The gopher's home looks like a huge subway with no lights. Everything is as dark as coal. But that suits the pocket gopher just fine. Its whiskers help it feel its way around.

The animal stops when its whiskers let it know roots are dangling overhead. The gopher pulls on them. An entire plant falls into the tunnel.

A gopher's tunnel is underground, so it has no light. The gopher must use its whiskers to feel its way around.

23

The gopher nibbles on a few leaves. Then it cuts the plant into pieces with its powerful teeth. Later, it will store the food in one of its side tunnels.

Every now and then, the gopher's whiskers wriggle in the air. The sensitive hairs feel for other roots sticking out. They also search for the presence of an enemy, such as a snake.

Sometimes the animal slips aboveground. If it has to make a fast getaway, it backs into its hole. Whiskers on its tail help it feel its way while running backward.

When the gopher reaches safety, it does a somersault. Whiskers on its nose then lead it deeper into the tunnel. Without its whiskers, the gopher would not be able to live where it does.

Once in a while, a gopher pokes its head aboveground. Its whiskers sweep the air for any sign of danger.

FOOD FINDERS

A walrus leaves its ice shelf and drops into the Arctic Sea. It swims deeper and deeper into dark, cold waters. It is searching for food.

No light shines on the sea bottom. But the walrus does not need light. Hundreds of stiff whiskers cover its upper lip like a mustache. With these hairs, the walrus can easily find its favorite seafood.

The walrus's nose and whiskers comb the mud and sand. Soon the walrus senses the hideout of clams. Whiskers sweep the sand to one side. But the clams are buried too deeply.

A walrus's whiskers are always busy finding and sweeping up food.

Next, the giant animal squirts a jet of water out of its mouth. The blast sends sand in every direction. Many delicious clams are now uncovered.

Whiskers quickly become **chopsticks**. They pick up a tasty clam, shell and all. The walrus sucks the clam out of its shell. It can eat as many as four thousand shellfish at one meal.

The walrus can stay underwater for about ten minutes. After that it swims to the surface for a breath of air. But soon its nose and whiskers are back searching the seafloor again.

The whiskers of a walrus feel like uncooked spaghetti.

WHISKER WARNING

An animal is sleeping high in a tree. Its legs are wrapped around a branch. Its tail covers its eyes.

As soon as the sky lightens, the creature begins to move. It lets out a loud *wha* sound. People in parts of China where it lives call the animal a wha. Red panda, *hun-ho,* and red cat bear are a few of its other names.

The red panda is a small relative of the giant panda. It is only about the size of a large house cat. It has whiskers like a cat and a tail like a raccoon.

The red panda spends most of its day sleeping and relaxing in trees.

During early morning or evening, the red panda hunts for food. It especially enjoys nibbling on tender leaves and shoots of **bamboo**. It also eats mushrooms, fruit, insects, and birds' eggs.

The red panda's eyesight and sense of smell are poor. When the animal is on the ground, its long white whiskers sweep the air. As soon as they sense danger, they send a signal to the animal's brain.

The next second, the red panda rushes up a tree. It wraps itself around a branch until it is almost invisible. There the animal stays hidden until its whiskers signal that it is safe to hunt again.

The red panda's whiskers help it search for food, such as bamboo leaves.

TRACKING FISH

An animal running across mud or sand leaves tracks. A fish swimming in water also leaves tracks. It makes tiny ripples called a **wake**. Many sea mammals follow wakes when they hunt prey in dark rivers or oceans.

Scientists wanted to find out how some animals follow wakes. They blindfolded two harbor seals and covered their ears so they could not hear. Then they placed a toy submarine in a large pool of water.

A boat leaves behind a wake when it speeds on water. This is like the wake of a fish but much larger.

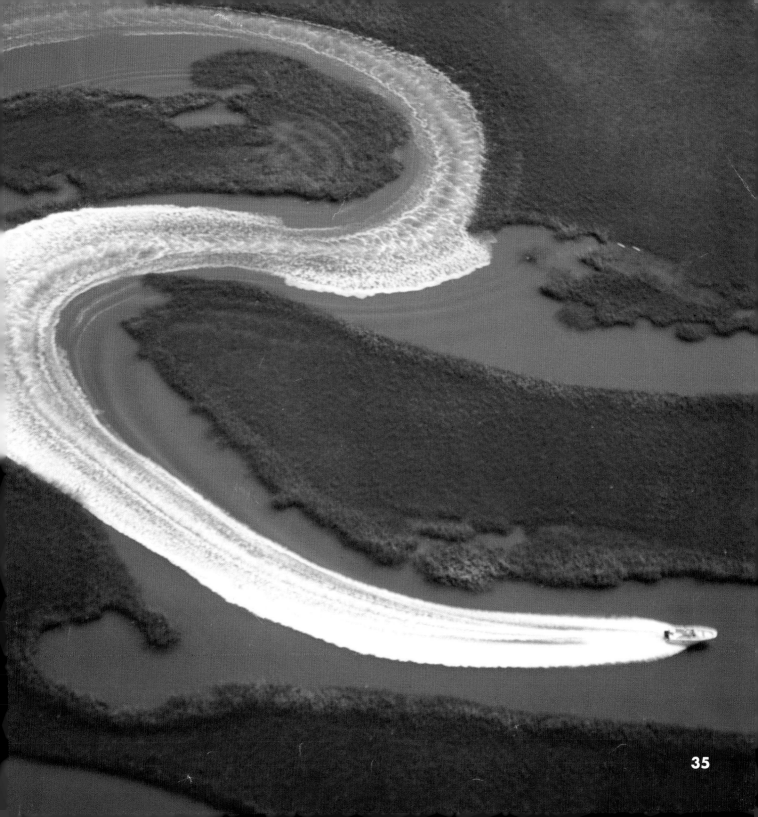

One seal began its search by pointing its whiskers forward. It moved its head back and forth until it found the sub's ripples. Then the seal stayed close behind the sub as it moved around the pool.

Both harbor seals were given the same test several times. Both were able to follow the sub. But the animals failed the test when their whiskers were covered. The scientists knew then that whiskers helped the seals follow wakes.

In the wild, harbor seals use their whiskers to follow the wakes of fish, shrimp, and squid (not toy subs).

MORE WHISKERS

The first hairs that grow on an unborn kitten's body are whiskers. When the animals are born, they are blind and deaf. But they can still explore the world around them. They do it with their whiskers.

Newborn kittens depend on their whiskers to learn about everything around them.

Pocket gophers and manatees are not the only mammals with whiskers in unusual places. Right whales have whiskers around their blowholes. These stiff hairs may help the animals feel the ripples of tiny creatures as they swim overhead.

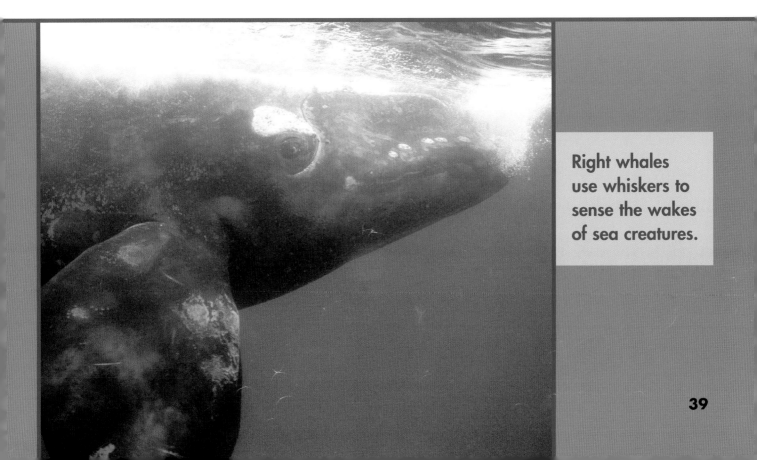

Right whales use whiskers to sense the wakes of sea creatures.

Flying squirrels have whiskers on their ankles as well as on their cheeks. As the animals leap from tree to tree, they cannot always see too well. Ankle whiskers detect branches where they can safely land.

Flying squirrels use their whiskers when leaping through the air.

Mammals are the only kind of animals with true whiskers. But if you have ever seen a whip-poor-will, you might wonder. The birds have long, stiff feathers around their beaks. Their feather whiskers help them trap and scoop bugs into their mouths.

Whip-poor-wills have whiskerlike feathers around their beaks.

41

Catfish also have whiskerlike growths around their mouths. These are known as **barbels**. Barbels are not made of hair like regular whiskers are. With barbels the catfish uncover food in dark or muddy waters.

Catfish look like they have whiskers around their mouths.

Young flying fish also have long whiskers around their mouths. The whiskers grow down from their jaws and are longer than the fish's body. They may help the animals locate food. But the whiskers disappear as the fish grow. No one is certain why. Call it the mystery of the disappearing whiskers.

Flying fish lose their whiskers as they get older.

GLOSSARY

bamboo: a kind of grass that has long, stiff stems and narrow leaves

barbels: whiskerlike growths on a fish

chopsticks: a pair of sticks used in some Asian countries for eating food

mammals: animals that have hair and feed their young with mother's milk

prey: an animal that is hunted and killed by another animal

vibrissae: scientific name for whiskers

wake: the ripples or tracks made by anything moving through water

FURTHER READING

BOOKS
Baillie, Marilyn. *Wild Talk.* Vancouver, BC: Maple Tree Press, 1996.

Bauman, Amy. *The Wonder of Manatees.* Milwaukee: Gareth Stevens Publishing, 2000.

Daly, Catherine. *Whiskers.* New York: Random House, 2000.

Dowswell, Paul. *First Encyclopedia of Animals.* London: Usborne Publishing, Ltd., 2002.

Lauber, Patricia. *The True-or-False Book of Cats.* Washington, DC: National Geographic Society, 1998.

Markle, Sandra. *Outside and Inside Rats.* New York: Atheneum Books, 2001.

Pipe, Jim. *Paws, Tails, and Whiskers.* Danbury, CT: Franklin Watts, 2004.

Staub, Frank J. *Walruses.* Minneapolis: Lerner Publications Company, 1999.

WEBSITES

Fort Wayne Children's Zoo
> http://www.kidszoo.com/animals/redpanda.htm
> Check out the photo of the red panda at the Fort Wayne
> Children's Zoo. Learn a few more facts about the animal.

Manatees
> http://www.oceanconservancy.org/site/PageServer?pagename=
>   fw_manatees
> Find out more about manatees at The Ocean Conservancy
> website.

National Geographic Kids
> http://www.nationalgeographic.com/ngkids/9706/wackyq.html
> Take a "Wacky Whiskers Quiz" at this National Geographic
> Kids website.

INDEX

Page numbers in *italics* refer to illustrations.

PHOTO ACKNOWLEDGMENTS

Images reproduced with permission from:
© Steven Kazlowski/Peter Arnold, Inc., p. 2; © Hans Reinhard/OKAPIA/Photo Researchers, Inc., p. 6; © Gerard Lacz/Peter Arnold, Inc., p. 9; © Tom McHugh/ Photo Researchers, Inc., pp. 11, 22; © Carlos Sanz/V&W/SeaPics.com, p. 12; © Gerard Lacz/Animals Animals, p. 15; © Robert Maier/Animals Animals, p. 16; © Robert Henno/Peter Arnold, Inc., p. 19; © Douglas Faulkner/Photo Researchers, Inc., p. 21; © Kenneth M. Highfill/Photo Researchers, Inc., p. 25; © Goran Ehlme/SeaPics.com, p. 27; © Johnny Johnson/Animals Animals, p. 28; © Fritz Polking; Frank Lane Picture Agency/CORBIS, p. 31; © Tim Davis/Photo Researchers, Inc., p. 32; © Alan Schein Photography/CORBIS, p. 35; © Gregory Ochocki/Photo Researchers, Inc., p. 36; © DK Limited/CORBIS, p. 38; © Hiroya Minakuchi/SeaPics.com, p. 39; © Nick Bergkessel Jr./Photo Researchers, Inc., p. 40; © Jim Grace/Photo Researchers, Inc., p. 41; © E. R. Degginger/Photo Researchers, Inc., p. 42; © Doug Perrine/SeaPics.com, p. 43.

Front cover: © Adam Jones/Visuals Unlimited.